PRACTICAL HANDBOOK OF INDUSTRIAL PHARMACY-I

Strictly as per P.C.I (R.G.P.V.) Syllabus Prescribed for B.pharmacy V Semester

Ms. Komal Tikariya

B.Pharm, M.Pharm

Assistant Professor

BM College of Pharmaceutical Education and Research, Indore

MadhyaPradesh, India

Mr.Umesh K. Atneriya

B.Pharm, M.Pharm, PhD[*]

Research Scholar

School of Pharmacy DAVV, Indore

Madhya Pradesh, India

NOTION PRESS

DEDICATION

This book is dedicated to our parents, family members, friends and almighty god.

S. No.	Title
Experiment no.1	Preformulation studies on paracetamol/Aspirin/or any other drug.
Experiment no.2	Preparation and evaluation of Paracetamol tablets.
Experiment no.3	Preparation and evaluation of Aspirin tablets.
Experiment no.4	Coating of tablets- film coating of tablets and granules.
Experiment no.5	Preparation and evaluation of Tetracycline capsules.
Experiment no.6	Preparation of Calcium Gluconate injection.
Experiment no.7	Preparation of Ascorbic Acid injection.
Experiment no.8	Quality control test of marketed tablets / capsules as per IP.
Experiment no.9	Preparation of Eye ointment.
Experiment no.10	Preparation of Chloramphenicol Eye ointment.
Experiment no.11	Preparation of Creams (cold cream).

Preface

Industrial Pharmacy is the branch of Pharmacy that deals with Scientific and technological aspects related to design and Development of dosage forms. The current curriculam implemented by Pharmacy council of India New Delhi as Regulation 2014 has practical industrial Pharmacy - I subject at semester – V of third year of the B.Pharm course. This practical book covers Whole of the experimental components Specified in the Syllabus. The book has been covering different dosage forms like tablets, capsules, injections, eye drops and eye ointment, creams .

We would like to thanks all our colleagues for their valuable suggestions to write this book in a simplest way for the Pharmacy students in a respective prescribed syllabus

Experiment No: 1

Aim: Preformulation study on paracetamol.

Reference:lackmann, Leon, libermann, Herbert; The theory and practice of Industrial Pharmacy; Varghese Pusblishing House, Edition Third, Page no. 171.

Requirement:

Apparatus Required- Weighing balance, weights, Bulk density apparatus, Butter paper, Tapped density apparatus, stop watch, distilled water, pipette, measuring cylinder.

Chemical Required - Purified water, Paracetamol.

Theory: Preformulation study is the foundation of developing robust formulation. it can be defined as a phase of research & development process for an investigation of physical and chemical properties of new drug substance alone or in combination with other excipients in order to development of safe and effective dosage form.

- The overall objective of preformulation testing is to generate information useful to the formulator:

- To formulate stable and effective dosage form

- To increased drug stability

- To improve drug bioavailability

- Reduce drug excipient incompatibility

Procedure:

Preformulation study:

I) Pre-compression evaluation parameters:

a) Angleof repose.

b) Bulk density.

c) Tapped density.

d) Hausner's ratio.

a) **Angle of repose:**

Apparatus/glass wares	Qty
Angle of repose apparatus/	1
Funnel	1
Burette stand	1

1. Place the funnel on a ring supported by stand.
2. Take 50 g of powder and pass through sieve no. 20.
3. Block the orifice of the funnel by thumb.
4. Fill the powder in the funnel and remove the thumb immediately.
5. Maintain the gap between the bottom of the funnel and top of the powder pile.
6. After emptying the powder from the funnel, measure the height of the pile and diameter.

Observation:

Temperature = t*c

Weight of powder =

Sieve size used =

Glidant	Concentration Of glidant			Height of pile	Average height	Diameter of pile			Average daimeter
	I	II	mean			I	II	mean	

Calculation: angle of repose,

$$\tan \vartheta = 2h/D = h/r$$

b) **Method:** Both loose bulk density (LBD) and tapped bulk density (TBD) were determined. A quantity of accurately weighed powder (bulk) from each formula, previously shaken to break any agglomerates formed was introduced into a 25ml measuring cylinder. After the initial volume was observed, the cylinder was allowed to fall under its own weight on to a hard surface from the height of 2.5cm at 2 sec interval. The taping was continued until no further change in volume was noted.

c) Compressibility index:

1. Take measuring cylinder of capacity 10 ml.

2. Place the measuring cylinder a plane.

3. Powder substance pass through sieve no. 20 before use.

4. Weigh amount of powder is added carefully using the glass funnel or using paper without washing materials.

5. Measure the volume of the powder, called as fluffy volume.

6. Tap the measuring cylinder using tapping apparatus or on the wooden surface or on the pad.

7. Record the volume obtained after 50 tapping for 50 times.

If you want to knowing the effect of tapping, record the volume after a fix tapping. (vol. of the powder after 5,10, 15,......50 tapping)

Observation:

1. Temperature (room temp) = $t*c$
2. **Weight of powder =Wg**
3. Initiall volume of the powder (fluffy vol) =**Vo**
4. Volume of the powder after 50 tapping 50 times =**Vt**

S.no.	Number of tapping	Volume of powder
1	00	Vo
2	10	
3	15	
4	20	
5	25	
6	30	
7	40	
8	50	Vt

Calculation: fluffy density of the powder = W/Vo

Tapped density = W/Vt

Compressibility index (%) = Tapped density – fluffy density/tapped density *100

d) **Bulk Sdensity: procedure:**

1. Take about 70g of powder and pass through sieve no. 20.

2. Accurately weigh about 50g.

3. Fill the powder in a 100 ml capacity measuring cylinder.

4. Fix the measuring cylinder on the bulk density apparatus.

5. Start the apparatus and control the tapping by the timer attached with the instrument.

6. Note the bulk volume after tapping.

7. Or the bulk volume is determined by dropping the cylinder on the wooden surface three-time height about 1 inch for 2 inches for 2 mins.

OR

1) Take about 50g of powder.

2) Fill the powder in a 100 ml capacity measuring cylinder.

3) Now, put the sample in measuring cylinder.

4) See the vol. of powder after tapping.

5) Now take the vol. after 3 times of tapping.

6) Repeat the similar procedure for 40, 30, 20 g of powder.

7) Take the mean of the obtained reading.

Observation:

Weight of the powder = m

Bulk volume of powder = V

Number of tapping =

Room temperature =

Calculation = bulk density = mass pf powder/ bulk volume of powder.

Result the bulk density of the powder is =   …. g/cm^3

  a) Hausner's ratio: Hausner's ratio is an indirect index of ease of powder flow.

It is calculated by the following formula.

Hausner's ratio = t/b

Where t is tapped density and b is bulk density

Result: Preformulation study on paracetamol was Performed.

Experiment No: 2

Aim: To Prepare and evaluate Paracetamol tablets.

Reference: lackmann, Leon, libermann, Herbert; The theory and practice of Industrial Pharmacy; Varghese Pusblishing House, Edition Third, Page no. 293.

Requirements:

Apparatus Required- Weighing balance, weights, Monsanto hardness tester, Butter paper, Friabilator.Disintegration apparatus, stop watch, distilled water, pipette, measuring cylinder, UV spectrophotometer etc.

Chemical Required - Purified water, Paracetamol, lactose mucilage and corn starch, glidant (talc) and lubricant (magnesium stearate).

Formula:

Excipient	Quantity
Paracetamol	71.4%
Lactose	19.6%
Binder	2%
Corn starch	5%
Talc	1%
Magnesium stearate	1.0

Theory: A tablet is a pharmaceutical dosage form. Tablets may be defined as the solid unit dosage form of medicament or medicaments with or without suitable excipients and prepared either by moulding or by compression. It comprises a mixture of active substances and excipients, usually in powder form, pressed or compacted from a powder into a solid dose. The excipients can include diluents, binders, or granulating agents, glidants, (flow aids) and lubricants, to ensure efficient tabletting; disintegrants to promote tablet break-up in the digestive tract; sweeteners or flavors to enhance taste; and pigments to make the tablets visually attractive.

Procedure: Wet granulation method of tablet manufacturing was employed with milled binding agent and water as the granulating liquid. Paracetamol, lactose mucilage and corn starch were blended to form a damp coherent mass which was screened through a sieve No 10 and dried at 60°c for one hour. Corn starch was divided into two and incorporated during wet blending and after drying of granules to act as an intragranular and extra granulardisintegrate.

Compression of granules: The granules were blended with the disintegrant (corn starch), glidant (talc) and lubricant (magnesium stearate). The blend was compressed using a single punch tableting machine with a punch diameter of 0.75 cm set at 933 Pa compression pressure. The die volume was to correspond to the weight of the tablet to ensure that 500 mg paracetamol is obtained.

Evaluations:

a. Weight Variation:

Weigh 20 tablets selected at random and determine their average weight. NMT 2 of the individual weights may deviate from the average weight by more than the percentage deviation given in the above table and none should deviate by more than twice that percentage.

Calculation:

Total weight of 20 tablets = x gm

Average weight of the tablet = Total wt/ No. Of tablets

Limits allowed is ± --------%

b. Hardness test:

Monsanto Hardness Tester:

It has a graduated scale, which gives the reading in Kg/sq cm. The tablet to be tested is placed between the spindle and the Anvil. The desired pressure needed to hold the tablet in position is applied by moving the screw knob in clockwise direction. The scale is moved so that the indicator is fixed at zero. The pressure is applied till the tablet breaks. The reading is noted, which indicates the pressure, which is needed to break the tablet. NMT4Kg/sqcm is the Pharmacopoeial limit.

Observation:

The breaking strength of the given tablet is _________Kg/sq cm.

c. Friability:

The apparatus consists of a plastic chamber, which is divided into two parts and it revolves at a speed of 25rpm. Twenty tablets are weighed and placed in the plastic chamber. The chamber is rotated for 4mts or 100 revolutions. During each revolution the tablet falls from a distance of 6 inch. The tablets are removed from the chamber after 100 revolutions and weighed. Loss in weight indicates friability. The tablets are considered to be good quality if the loss in weight is less than 0.5 to 1%

Calculation:

Initial weight of 20 tablets (b)   = ----- gm

Final weight of 20 tablets   (a)   =   -------gm

Friability   = 100(1- a/b)   = -----%

The weight loss of the given tablet is ----------%

CONSOLIDATED REPORT:

TEST	OBSERVATION	STANDARD	INFERENCE
Weight variation	Average Wt = Lower Limit = Upper Limit =	%Deviation Lower Limit = Upper Limit =	
Hardness		NLT 4Kg/sqcm	
Friability		NMT 1%w/w	

(a) Disintegration Time:

For the Bioavailability of the dosage form it is very important that it should disintegrate, dissolve and enter into systemic circulation by absorption for its desired action. It provides greater surface area, which in turn increases the absorption.Disintegration means to break the tablets into smaller particles after swallowing.

"The time required to disintegrate the tablet is called disintegration time". The rate of disintegration depends upon the type of Tablet.

(b) Dissolution Test:

Dissolution plays an important role in the bioavailability of the drug. Since the absorption and physiological availability of the drug depends on its dissolved state. So it is important factor for a satisfactory tablet.

Procedure:

(a) Disintegration Time:

Place one tablet in each of the 6 tubes of the basket. Add a disc to each tube and operate the apparatus, using water maintained at $37°\pm2°$ as the immersion liquid. At the end of 15 min or after the time specified in the individual monograph, lift the basket from the liquid and observe the tablets. The tablet passes the test if all the six tablets have disintegrated. In case of one or two tablets fails to disintegrate repeat the test on 12 additional tablets. The tablet passes the test if NLT 16 of the tablets from the total 18 tablets tested has disintegrated and should comply the test.

TYPE OF TABLETS	TIME (min)	TEMPERATURE
Uncoated	15	
Film coated	30	
Enteric coated	120	
Dispersible	3	
Soluble	3	
Other		

(b). Dissolution Test:

Place 900ml of water, which should be free from dissolved air or as specified in the individual, monograph and previously warmed. Place one tablet in each of the six baskets in the vessel. Set the apparatus and start the motor and adjust the rotating speed to 100rpm for 45 min. After the time is completed, withdraw the solution, filter and determine the amount of active ingredients present through absorbance.

NLT 85% of the drug should be released. Repeat the operations for 5 times.

Observation:

Absorbance of test   =

Standard absorbance   =

Calculation:

% drug release =

Report:

TEST	OBSERVATION	STANDARD	INFERENCE
Disintegration Time			
Dissolution			

Result: The Paracetamol Tablet was Prepared and Evaluated.

Experiment No: 3

Aim: Preparation and evaluation of Aspirin tablets.

Reference:

1.Baboots, Sanjula; Ahuja, Alka; Ali, Javed; Industrial pharmaceutical technology; Birla publications Pvt ltd, page no. 21

2. lackmann, Leon, libermann, Herbert; The theory and practice of Industrial Pharmacy; Varghese Pusblishing House, Edition Third, Page no. 293.

Requirements:

Apparatus Required- Weighing balance, weights, Monsanto hardness tester, Butter paper, Friabilator. Disintegration apparatus, purified water, tablets, stop watch, distilled water, pipette, measuring cylinder, UV spectrophotometer etc.

Chemical Required – Aspirin, Citric Acid, Calcium Carbonate, Saccharin Sodium, Starch, Talc. Magnesium Stearate, Lactose.

Formula:

Ingredient	Quantity per tablet
Aspirin	0.3 g
Citric acid	0.03g
Calcium Carbonate	0.1 g
Saccharin sodium	3 g
Starch (4%)	20 mg
Talc (2.5%)	12.5 mg
Magnesium Stearate (1%)	5 mg
Diluent (Lactose)	500 mg

Theory: A tablet is a pharmaceutical dosage form. Tablets may be defined as the solid unit dosage form of medicament or medicaments with or without suitable excipients and prepared either by moulding or by compression. It comprises a mixture of active substances and excipients, usually in powder form, pressed or compacted from a powder into a solid dose. The excipients can include diluents, binders, or granulating agents, glidants, (flow aids) and lubricants, to ensure efficient tabletting; disintegrants to promote tablet break-up in the digestive tract; sweeteners or flavors to enhance taste; and pigments to make the tablets visually attractive.

Procedure:

1. Granulate Aspirin, Citric acid, diluent chosen (lactose) and disintegrant (starch) using non-aqueous binder
2. Pass the damp mass through sieve no. 8 and completely dry at 60 *c.
3. Pass the granules through sieve no. 20. Superimposed on sieve no. 44.
4. Take the granules which passes through sieve no. 20 and retained on sieve 44.
5. Mix the granules with glidant and anti-adherent and compress into tablets.
6. Subject the tablet to disintegration, friability, weight variation, and hardness tests.

Evaluation:

Friability:

Friability Roche friabilator is the equipment which is used for the determination of friability. It is expressed in percentage. Note down the initial weight of the tablets individually (W initial). Tablets are placed in a plastic chamber which revolves at 25 rpm and they are subjected to fall from a height of 6 inches in the friabilator for about 100 revolutions. Then measure the weight of the tablet (W final) and observe any weight difference before tablet and after the friabilator processing Limits: loss in weight less than 0.5 to 1% of the initial weight of the tablet should be considered as acceptable limits.

Disintegration test

In vitro disintegration test Disintegration is defined as the process of breakdown of tablet into small particles. Disintegration time of a tablet is determined by using disintegration test apparatus as per IP specifications. Place each tablet in each 6 tubes of the disintegration apparatus a then add a disc to each tube containing 6.8 pH phosphate buffer. The temperature of the buffer should maintain at $37 \pm 2°C$ and run the apparatus raised and lowered for 30 cycles per minute. Note down the time taken for the complete disintegration of the tablet without any remitants.

Weight variation test:

S.no.	Weight of Tablets	S.no.	Weight of Tablets
1		11	
2		12	
3		13	
4		14	
5		15	
6		16	
7		17	
8		18	
9		19	
10		20	

Weight of 20 tablets =

Average weight of a tablets = Total weight/20

Weight variation allowed according to IP/BP/USP =

Range =

Disintegration test-

S.NO.	Disintegration time
1	
2	
3	
4	
5	

Number of tablets used =

Medium =

Temperature =

Average Disintegration time =

Limit according to IP/BP/USP =

Friability test

Initial weight of 6 tablets =

Final weight of 6 tablets after friability testing =

% loss of weight = Initial weight – final weight/ initial weight *100

Limit =

Hardness

S.no.	Hardness (kg/cm2)
1	
2	
3	

Limits according to IP/BP/USP =

Thickness

S.No	Thickness
1	
2	
3	
4	
5	
6	
7	
8	
9	
10	

Average thickness =

Result

Prepared soluble aspirin tablets showed the following result:

1. Thickness =................ (cm/mm)

2. Weight variation = ...(pass/fail)

3. Disintegration= ....(pass/fail)

4. Friability= ....(pass/fail)

5. Hardness =............... (pass/fail)

Storage- Store below 25%

Store in well closed container

Protect from moisture Protect from moisture

Experiment No: 4

Aim: To perform Coating of tablets- film coating of tables/granules.

Reference: Baboots, Sanjula;, Ahuja, Alka; Ali, Javed; "Industrial pharmaceutical technology", edition 2004, Birla publications Pvt ltd, page no. 21

Requirement-

Apparatus Required= Beaker, Weighing machine, Measuring Cylinder, Spray Gun, Coating Pan.

Chemical Required= Aspirin, Ethyl cellulose solution (5 % in ethanol), Starch, Talc, Magnesium stearate, Lactose, Coating solution (eudragit l- 100 % solution in ethyl alcohol), Erythrocin solution.

Theory: Tablet coating is one of the oldest pharmaceutical processes still is existence. Coating is a process by which an essentially dry, outer layer of coating material is applied to the surface of a dosage form in order to confer specific benefits over uncoated variety. It involves application of a sugar or polymeric coat on the tablet. The advantages of tablet coating are taste masking, odor masking, physical and chemical protection, protects the drug in the stomach, and to control its release profile. There are several techniques for tablet coating such as sugar coating, film coating and enteric coating. The disadvantages of the older techniques of coating have been overcome with the recent advancement in coating technologies. In these technologies coating materials are directly applied on the surface of the tablet without the use of any solvent. ICH guidelines also prefer the avoidance of organic solvents in pharmaceutical dosage formulations considering products safety profile. This review discusses the basic concepts of tablet coating, the recent advancements made, the problem faced during the process, their solutions and coating evaluation.

S.no.	Ingredients	Quantity per tablet (mg)
	Aspirin	325
	Ethyl cellulose solution (5 % in ethanol)	20
	Starch	20
	Talc	20
	Magnesium stearate	8
	Lactose	7

	Coating solution (eudragit l- 100 % solution in ethyl alcohol)	
	Erythrocin solution	1 ml

Procedure:

1. Add ethyl cellulose solution to aspirin to form a coherent mass. Granulate and dry the granules. place 40g of granules into a beaker and rotate in a ball mill at 75 rpm.
2. Spray the coating solution with the help of spray gun.
3. Dry the granulesin a current of hot air.
4. Repeat the process several times so as to obtain desired coating thickness.

Storage: Store in cool and dry place

Result: The given product was prepared and submitted

Experiment No: 5

Aim: Preparation and evaluation of Tetracycline capsules.

Reference: lackmann, Leon, libermann, Herbert; The theory and practice of Industrial Pharmacy; Varghese Pusblishing House, Edition Third, Page no. 374.

Requirement:

Apparatus Required- Weighing balance, weights, Disintegration apparatus, stop watch, distilled water, pipette, measuring cylinder.

Chemical Required: Tetracycline Hydrochloride, Lactose

Theory: In the manufacture of pharmaceuticals, **encapsulation** refers to a range of dosage form—techniques used to enclose medicines—in a relatively stable shell known as a **capsule**, allowing them to, for example, be taken orally or be used as suppositories. The two main types of capsules are:

- Hard-shelled capsules, which contain dry, powdered ingredients or miniature pellets made by *e.g.* processes of extrusion or spheronization. These are made in two halves: a smaller-diameter "body" that is filled and thesn sealed using a larger-diameter "cap".
- Soft-shelled capsules, primarily used for oils and for active ingredients that are dissolved or suspended in oil.

Different sizes of capsules and volume filled in ml

S.no.	Capsule no	Volume in ml
1.	000	1.36
2.	00	0.95
3.	0	0.67
4.	1	0.48
5.	2	0.37
6.	3	0.27
7.	4	0.20
8.	5	0.13

Formula:

Ingredient	Quantity
Choroteracycline/ tetracycline hcl	250mg

| Diluent | Qs |

Each capsule will contain

Tetracycline Hydrochloride..........250mg

Procedure:

1. Calculate the quantity of drug substances and diluent by formulaand calculate the quantity of one extra capsule.
2. Select the capsule size as per requirements.
3. Fill the capsule carefully by hand operating machine or manually with minimum weight variations.

Calculations:

for example: A formulation has theoretical weight 325 mg and tapped and bulk density of a substance 0.75 g/ml while bulk density of inert substance is 0.80g/ml.

Given

1. Weight of substance in each capsule = 325.0 mg
2. Bulk density of substance = 0.75 g/ml
3. Bilk density of inert substance = 0.80 g/ml

Volume occupied by fill weight = weight of substance in each capsule/ bulk density of substance   = 0.325/0.75 = 0.43 ml

Volume size of one capsule = 0.48 ml (by table)

Volume occupied by drug = 0.43ml (by calculation)

Volume unoccupied = 0.48 -0.43= 0.05 ml

Weight of diluent or inert substance = volume * bulk density

= 0.05*0.80 = 0.040g= 40.0mg

Send ten capsules of given materials

Weight for 11 capsules of substance = 325 *11 = 3.575 g

Weight of diluent or inert substance = 40 *11 = 0.440 g

Total weight of filling substance in hard empty shell = 4.015 g

Evaluation:

1. Weight variation- Determine by simple weighing of 20 tablets using digital balance, should be within the limit of 90 % to 110% in weight.
2. Disintegration- Disintegration test is usually not required for capsules unless it istreated to resist solution in gastric fluid. In such cases it must meet the requirement for disintegration of enteric coated tablets.
3. Dissolution test: Use dissolution apparatus basket assembly for determination of dissolution test.

Weight variation test:

S.no.	Weight of Tablets	S.no.	Weight of Tablets
1		11	
2		12	
3		13	
4		14	
5		15	
6		16	
7		17	
8		18	
9		19	
10		20	

4. Weight of 20 tablets =
5. Average weight of a capsules = Total weight/20

6. Weight variation allowed according to IP/BP/USP =

7. Range =

Disintegration test

S.NO.	Disintegration time
1	
2	
3	

1. Number of capsules used =

2. Medium =

3. Temperature =

4. Average Disintegration time =

5. Limit according to IP/BP/USP =

Category: Antibiotic

Dose: 1-3 Tablets daily in divided doses.

Storage: Preserve choroteracycline capsule in a well closed container in a cool place. Temperature not exceeding 30*c.

Uses: Antiprotozoal preparation

Result: Tetracycline capsules was Prepared and evaluated.

Experiment No: 6

Object: Preparation of Calcium Gluconate injection.

Reference: Subramanyam, C.V.S; laboratory manual of industrial pharmacy; Vallabh publications, Page no. 153

Requirement:

As per IP

Ingredients	Official formula
Calcium gluconate	9.65 g
Calcium D- sacchrate	0.35 g
Water for injection	100 ml qs

Appratus	Qty
Ampoules	100
Beaker 250 ml	1
Beaker 100 ml	1
Measuring cylinder 10 ml	1
Syringe with needle 10 ml	1
Whattmann filter	1
Autoclave	1

Theory: Calcium is the fifth most abundant element in the body and is essential for maintenance of the functional integrity of nervous, muscular, skeletal systems and cell membrane and capillary permeability. It is also an important activator in many enzymatic reactions and is essential to a number of physiologic processes including transmission of nerve impulses; contraction of cardiac, smooth and skeletal muscles; renal function; respiration and blood coagulation. Calcium also plays regulatory roles in the release and storage of neurotransmitters and hormones, in the uptake and binding of amino acids, and in cyanocobalamin (vitamin B12) absorption and gastric secretion.

Calcium gluconate is used to treat conditions arising from calcium deficiencies such as hypercalcaemic tetany, hypocalcaemia related to hypoparathyroidism and hypocalcaemia due to rapid growth or pregnancy. It is also used in the treatment of black widow spider bites to relieve muscle cramping and as an adjunct in the treatment of rickets, osteomalacia, lead colic and magnesium sulphate overdosage.

Calcium gluconate has also been employed to decrease capillary permeability in allergic conditions, nonthrombocytopenic purpura and exudative dermatoses such as dermatitis herpetiformis and for pruritus of eruptions caused by certain drugs. In hyperkalaemia, calcium gluconate may aid in antagonizing the cardiac toxicity provided the patient is not receiving digitalis therapy.

CONTRAINDICATIONS

Calcium salts are contraindicated in patients with ventricular fibrillation or hypercalcemia. Intravenous administration of calcium is contraindicated when serum calcium levels are above normal.

Procedure:

1. Cleaning of ampules in type 1 glass
2. The desired amount of calcium gluconate and calcium D saccharate are accurately weighed.
3. On account of solubility problems, calcium gluconate is first dissolved in water for injection in beaker with the aid of heat.
4. Then calcium D- saccharate is dissolved in the above solution.
5. The solution is allowed to cool.
6. After cooling, the drug solution is filtered through G-4 filter (or whattmann filter paper) to remove any foreign particles.
7. Sealing of ampoules: the ampules can be sealed by using pull sealing technique.
8. Sterilization can be achieved by autoclaving at 121*c for 30 mins.

Dose: 1 to 2 g (500 mg of calcium gluconate is approx. equivalent to 2.3 mmol of ca++)

Storage: store in a cool and dry place

Routes of administration: Intra muscular or slow intra venous.

Date of expiry: 3 years from the date of mfg.

Each ml contains 100 mg of total calcium

Auxiliary labels: Discard if any particulate is present. If any crystallization occurs during storage. The injection must clear at the time of use.

Experiment No: 7

Aim: Preparation of Ascorbic Acid injection.

Reference: Subramanyam, C.V.S; laboratory maLOL;P0nual of industrial pharmacy; Vallabh publications, page no. 151

Requirement:

Formula: As per IP

Each ml contains Ascorbic Acid 500 mg

Ingredients	Quantity
Ascorbic acid	25.00 g
Sodium bicarbonate	14.58 g
p-chloro meta cresol	0.1 g
Water for injection	Qs 100ml

Apparatus:

Apparatus	Qty
Ampoules	100
Beaker 250 ml	1
Beaker 100 ml	1
Measuring cylinder 10 ml	1
Syringe with needle 10 ml	1
Whattmann filter	1
Autoclave	1

Theory:

Ascorbic Acid (vitamin C) is a water-soluble vitamin. It occurs as a white or slightly yellow crystal or powder with a light acidic taste. It is an antiscorbutic product. On exposure to air and light it gradually darkens. In the dry state it is reasonably stable in air, but in solution it rapidly oxidizes. Ascorbic Acid is freely soluble in water; sparingly soluble in alcohol; insoluble in chloroform, ether, and benzene. The chemical name of Ascorbic Acid is L-ascorbic acid. The molecular formula is C 6H 80 6 and the molecular weight is 176.13.

The structural formula is as follows:

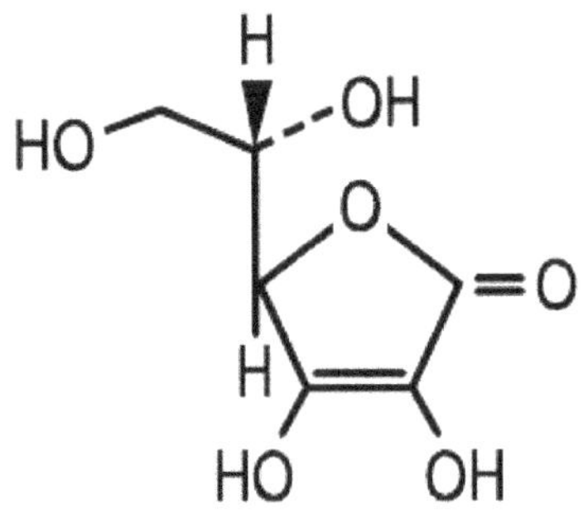

Procedure:

1. 2/3 of the total volume of water is placed in a beaker.
2. Ascorbic acid is weighed and suspended in water with continuous stirring.
3. Sodium bicarbonate is slowly added with vigorous stirring, effervescence is produced.
4. After subsiding the effervescence, remaining sodium bicarbonate is added. This process is continued till ascorbic acid completely dissolves.
5. Para choloro-meta cresol is added and stirred to dissolve.
6. The pH is adjusted to 5.7.
7. The solution is filtered through G-4/ whattmann filter.

Sterilization:the sealed ampoules are sterilized by steaming for 30 mins.

Composition: Each ml contains 250 mg of ascorbic acid.

Category: Antiscorbutic (ascorbic acid is used in the prevention and treatment of scurvy)

Dose: Prohylacticdose: 25 – 75 mg daily.

Therapeutic dose- not less than 250 mg daily in divided dose.

Storage: store in a cool and dry place

Routes of administration: Intra muscular.

Date of expiry: 2 years from the date of mfg.

Auxiliary labels: Discard of any particulate is present

If any crystallization occurs during storage, warming may dissolve a precipitate. The injection must clear at the time of use.

Result: The ascorbic Acid injection was prepared and submitted

Experiment No: 8

Aim: Quality control test of (as per IP) marketed tablets and capsules.

Reference:lackmann, Leon, libermann, Herbert; The theory and practice of Industrial Pharmacy;

Varghese Pusblishing House, Edition Third, Page no. 293 and 374.

Requirement:

Apparatus Required = Weighing balance, weights, Monsanto hardness tester, Butter paper, Friabilator. Disintegration apparatus, purified water, tablets, stop watch, distilled water, pipette, measuring cylinder, UV spectrophotometer etc.

Theory: A tablet is a pharmaceutical dosage form. Tablets may be defined as the solid unit dosage form of medicament or medicaments with or without suitable excipients and prepared either by moulding or by compression. It comprises a mixture of active substances and excipients, usually in powder form, pressed or compacted from a powder into a solid dose. The excipients can include diluents, binders, or granulating agents, glidants, (flow aids) and lubricants, to ensure efficient tabletting; disintegrants to promote tablet break-up in the digestive tract; sweeteners or flavors to enhance taste; and pigments to make the tablets visually attractive.

In the manufacture of pharmaceuticals, **encapsulation** refers to a range of dosage form—techniques used to enclose medicines—in a relatively stable shell known as a **capsule**, allowing them to, for example, be taken orally or be used as suppositories. The two main types of capsules are:

- Hard-shelled capsules, which contain dry, powdered ingredients or miniature pellets made by *e.g.* processes of extrusion or spheronization. These are made in two halves: a smaller-diameter "body" that is filled and thesn sealed using a larger-diameter "cap".
- Soft-shelled capsules, primarily used for oils and for active ingredients that are dissolved or suspended in oil.

Evaluation:

Friability:

Friability Roche friabilator is the equipment which is used for the determination of friability. It is expressed in percentage. Note down the initial weight of the tablets individually (W initial). Tablets are placed in a plastic chamber which revolves at 25 rpm and they are subjected to fall from a height of 6 inches in the friabilator for about 100 revolutions. Then measure the weight of the tablet (W final) and observe any weight difference before tablet and after the friabilator processing Limits: loss in weight less than 0.5 to 1% of the initial weight of the tablet should be considered as acceptable limits.

Disintegration test

In vitro disintegration test Disintegration is defined as the process of breakdown of tablet into small particles. Disintegration time of a tablet is determined by using disintegration test apparatus as per IP specifications. Place each tablet in each 6 tubes of the disintegration apparatus a then add a disc to each tube containing 6.8 pH phosphate buffer. The temperature of the buffer should maintain at $37 \pm 2°C$ and run the apparatus raised and lowered for 30 cycles per minute. Note down the time taken for the complete disintegration of the tablet without any remitants.

Weight variation test:

S.no.	Weight of Tablets	S.no.	Weight of Tablets
1		11	
2		12	
3		13	
4		14	
5		15	
6		16	
7		17	
8		18	
9		19	
10		20	

Weight of 20 tablets =

Average weight of a tablets = Total weight/20

Weight variation allowed according to IP/BP/USP =

Range =

Disintegration test-

S.NO.	Disintegration time
1	
2	
3	
4	
5	

Number of tablets used =

Medium =

Temperature =

Average Disintegration time =

Limit according to IP/BP/USP =

Friability test

Initial weight of 6 tablets =

Final weight of 6 tablets after friability testing =

% loss of weight = Initial weight – final weight/ initial weight *100

Limit =

Hardness

S.no.	Hardness (kg/cm2)
1	
2	
3	

Limits according to IP/BP/USP =

Thickness

S.No	Thickness
1	
2	
3	
4	
5	
6	
7	
8	
9	
10	

Average thickness =

Test:

1. Appearance

2. Size and Shape

3. Unique Identification Markings

4. Content Uniformity Test

5. Mass Variation Test

6. Disintegration Test

7. Dissolution Test

8. Stability Test

Procedure : Same as evaluation of tablets experiment 2 and 5.

Experiment No: 9

Object: Preparation of Simple Eye ointment.

Reference: Gaud, R.S.; Gupta, G.D; practical pharmaceutic, CBS publishers and distributors, page no. 142

Requirements:

Chemical Required:

Ingredient	Quantity
Wool fat	10.0 g
Yellow soft paraffin	80.0g
Liquid paraffin, sufficient to produce	100.0g

Glassware Required:

Appratus/ glassware	Qty
Beaker	1
Funnel	1
Filter paper- coarse	1
Hot air own	1
Aluminium foil	Qs

Theory:

Eye ointments: Eye ointments are sterile, semi-solid preparations of homogenous appearance intended for application to the eye. They may contain one or more medicaments dissolved or dispersed in a suitable basis. Bases, which are usually nonaqueous, may contain suitable auxiliary substances such as stabilizing agents, antimicrobial preservatives and antioxidants. The base selected must be non-irritant to the conjunctiva, allow the drug to diffuse throughout the secretions of the eye and retain the activity of the medicaments for a reasonable period of time under the stated conditions of storage.

Procedure:

1. Melt together weight amount of wool fat and yellow soft paraffin in a container.
2. Add liquid paraffin to make up weight 100g.
3. Filter the hot mixture coarse filter paper placed in a heated funnel.
4. Filtrate is sterilized by dry heat at 150*c for sufficient time to ensure that the whole is maintained at this temperature for one hour.
5. Allow to cool at room temperature without opening the container.

Storage: 5.0 g in small sterilized collapsible tube with the stated strength should be dispensed unless otherwise directed. Eye ointment may be unstable and should be stored in a cool place.

Uses: Pharmaceutical aid

Category: Pharmaceutical aid

Result: The simple eye ointment was prepared and submitted.

Experiment No: 10

Object: Preparation of Chloramphenicol Eye ointment.

Reference: Gaud, R.S.; Gupta, G.D; practical pharmaceutic, CBS publishers and distributors, page no. 143

Requirement:

Chemical Required:

Ingredient	Quantity
Chloramphenicol	0.2g
Simple eye ointment	10.0g

Glassware Requirements:

Apparatus/ glassware	Qty
Beaker	1
Glass rode	1
Aluminum foil	Qs

Theory:

Eye ointments: Eye ointments are sterile, semi-solid preparations of homogenous appearance intended for application to the eye. They may contain one or more medicaments dissolved or dispersed in a suitable basis. Bases, which are usually nonaqueous, may contain suitable auxiliary substances such as stabilizing agents, antimicrobial preservatives and antioxidants. The base selected must be non-irritant to the conjunctiva, allow the drug to diffuse throughout the secretions of the eye and retain the activity of the medicaments for a reasonable period of time under the stated conditions of storage.

Procedure:

1. Triturate chloramphenicol with simple eye ointment in aseptic conditions.
2. Add sufficient quantity of sterile simple eye ointment.

Storage: Eye ointment may be unstable and should be stored in a cool place.

Uses: Anti- microbial or infection

Category: Antibiotic

Result: The given product is prepared and submitted.

Experiment No: 11

Object: To prepare and submit 15 gm of Cold cream.

Reference: R. S. Gaud and G. D. Gupta, 2002, Practical Pharmaceutics, 1st Ed., CBS Publication, PP.32. Kasture P.V. and Gokhale S. B. 2015, Practical Pharmaceutics-I, 21st Ed. Nirali Prakashan,PP.6.3.

Requirement:

Apparatus- Beaker (100 ml), Measuring Cylinder (50 ml), Pipette, spatula, Water bath.

Chemical- Bees Wax, Liquid paraffin, Borax Methyl Paraben, Propyl Paraben, Perfume, Purified water.

Theory:

In this bees wax-borax type preparation borax reacts with the free fatty acids present in the beeswax and produces soft soap which acts as the emulsifying agent and emulsifies the oil phase containing bees wax, mineral oil, paraffin etc. in the aqueous phase.

During formulation heated aqueous phase is added to oil phase, addition of oily phase toaqueous phase, it results in clump formation.

Category: Emollient and cleansing cream.

Storage: store in well closed container

FORMULATION TABLE:

Ingredient	QuantityGiven	Quantity Taken (Factor x Q. G.)	Use of Ingredient
Beeswax	16 gm		
Liquid paraffin	50 gm		
Borax	0.8 gm		
Methyl paraben	0.18 gm		
Propyl paraben	0.02 gm		
Perfume	q.s.		
Purified water (q.s)	33 ml		

Procedure:

1. Melt beeswax, liquid paraffin and propyl paraben in order of increasing melting point.

2. Dissolve methyl paraben, borax in water at 75*c. filter if required.Add aqueous phase to oil phase with continuous stirring

3. Cool with stirring to room temperature

4. Add perfume to the preparation at room temperature.

5. Transfer the cream to the container while hot.

Result: The given product is prepared and submitted.

ABOUT THE AUTHORS

Ms. Komal Tikariya; B. Pharm, M.Pharm (Pharmaceutics) has worked on the research related to the Novel drug delivery system. Currently working as Assistant professor in BM College of Pharmaceutical Education and Research, Indore, Madhya Pradesh, India. She has 5 year of Experience in Teaching.

Mr.Umesh K. Atneriya; B. Pharm, M.Pharm (Pharmaceutics), PhD *has worked on the research related to the solubility enhancement of drug. Currently working as Associate professor in BM College of Pharmaceutical Education and Research, Indore, Madhya Pradesh, India. he has 12 year of Experience in Teaching.

www.ingramcontent.com/pod-product-compliance
Lightning Source LLC
Chambersburg PA
CBHW040218110726
48005CB00019B/3073